POLAR

WILDLIFE

D0598687

a Joshua Morris book
from The Reader's Digest Association, Inc.

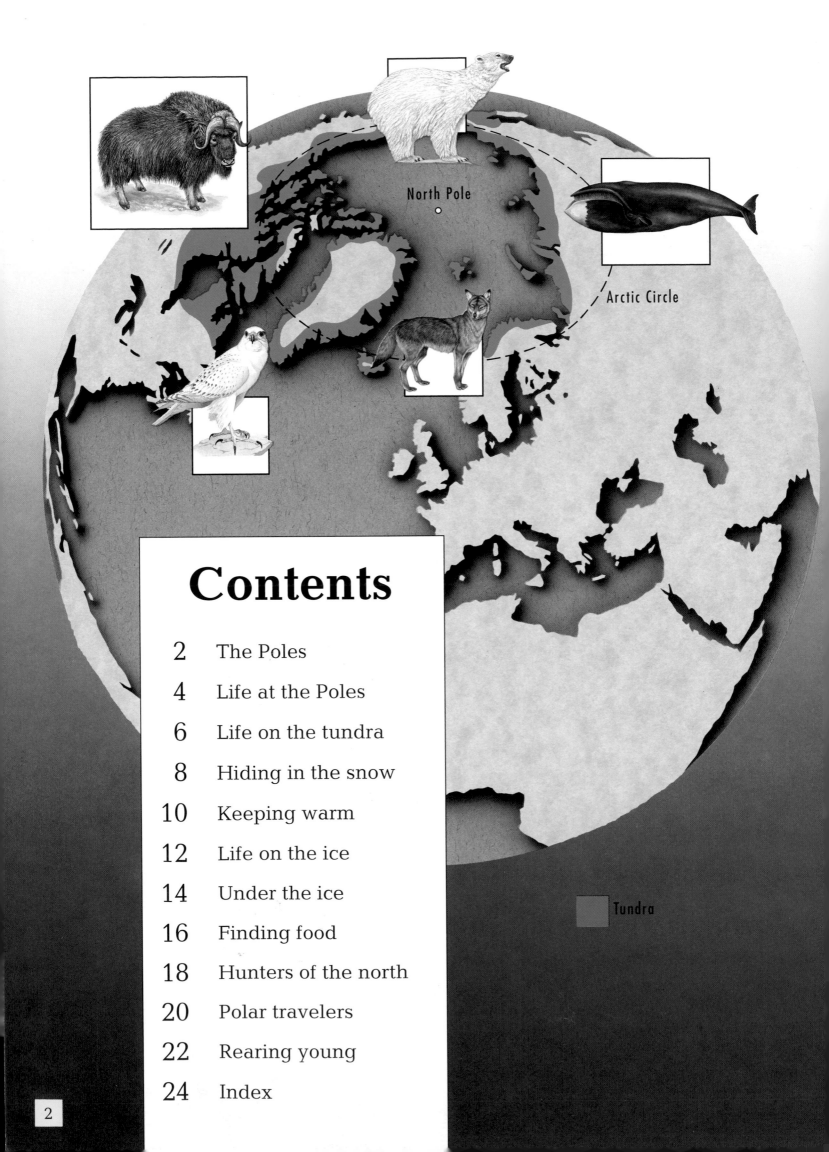

North Pole

Arctic Circle

Tundra

Contents

2   The Poles

4   Life at the Poles

6   Life on the tundra

8   Hiding in the snow

10   Keeping warm

12   Life on the ice

14   Under the ice

16   Finding food

18   Hunters of the north

20   Polar travelers

22   Rearing young

24   Index

The Poles

THE EXTREME ENDS of the earth, the North Pole and the South Pole, are bitterly cold. Here the snow never melts and the sea is covered with ice. The region around the North Pole is called the Arctic. Most of this area is sea, but at its center there is a huge mass of floating ice nearly 2,000 miles across. The northern lands bordering the Arctic Ocean are known as tundra.

Antarctica, the area around the South Pole, is very different. It is a huge land continent with towering mountain ranges, all covered with thick layers of snow and ice.

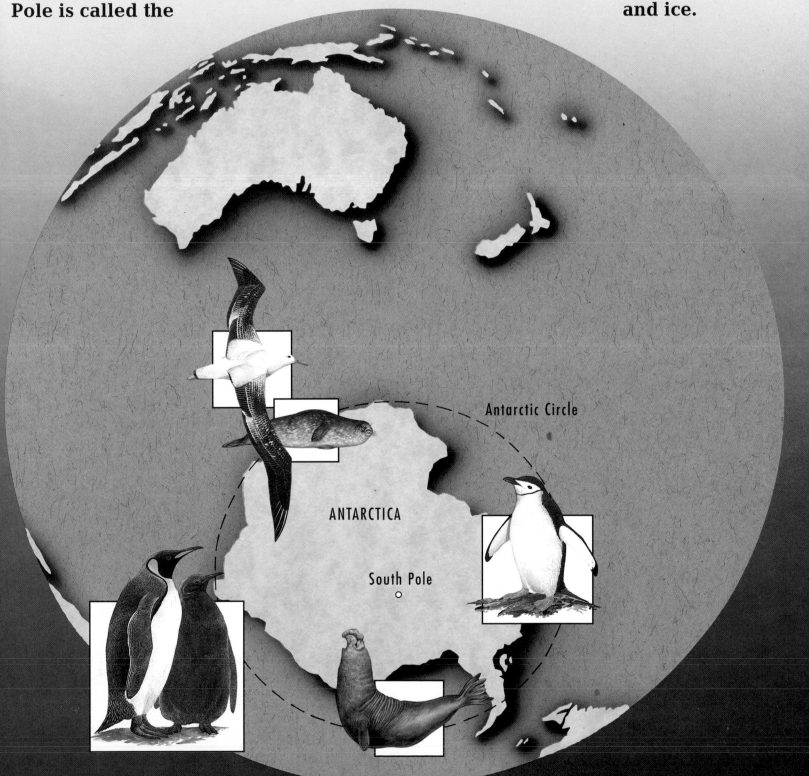

Antarctic Circle

ANTARCTICA

South Pole

Life in the Arctic

ON THE FROZEN polar ice cap itself, there are few plants or insects. But animals do manage to live there, catching fish or hunting one another. These animals, such as polar bears and seals, have thick coats of fur or layers of fatty blubber that help protect them from the cold. Many seabirds visit the Arctic, but usually only in the brief summer.

Life in the Antarctic

ANTARCTICA IS the coldest place on earth, with fierce winds and stormy seas. Temperatures there can go as low as –120°F. No land animals live on Antarctica except a few tiny insects like mites—the biggest of these is only half an inch long. But there is plenty of food in Antarctic seas for birds like penguins and for the many types of seals and whales.

Key

These pictures show some of the animals and birds that live in the Arctic and the Antarctic. In nature, they would not all be seen together. The Arctic tern migrates between the Arctic and the Antarctic.

1 Snow goose
2 Graylag goose
3 Arctic wolf
4 Ermine
5 Polar bear
6 Harp seal
7 Walrus
8 Arctic fox
9 Narwhal
10 Puffin
11 Ptarmigan
12 Arctic tern
13 Killer whale
14 Elephant seal
15 Skua
16 Fur seal
17 Emperor penguin
18 Chinstrap penguin
19 Adélie penguin
20 Gentoo penguin
21 King penguin and young
22 Storm petrel
23 Wandering albatross

Life on the tundra

THE COLD, BARE LANDS at the edges of the Arctic Ocean are known as the tundra. No trees survive the fierce winds that blow here, but some small ground-hugging plants grow in the short summer. These plants are food for animals such as lemmings and caribou. Many birds come to the tundra during the Arctic summer, but they fly south again in the harsh winter months.

Key

Some typical tundra animals are shown in this picture. In nature, of course, these animals would not all be seen together.

1	Arctic hare	7	Musk ox
2	Caribou	8	Ptarmigan
3	Tundra swan	9	Arctic ground squirrel
4	Gyrfalcon	10	Lemming
5	Snow bunting	11	Ermine (summer coat)
6	Wolverine		

Hiding in the snow

IN THE SNOWY WASTES of the polar regions there are no trees and very few places for animals to hide from their enemies or to lie in wait for prey. The best way to keep out of sight is to blend into the background. That's why so many polar animals and birds have white fur or feathers. This makes them hard to see in the snowy landscape. Imagine how easy it would be to spot a parrot in the Arctic!

In summer, **ptarmigans'** feathers are mottled browns and grays. In winter, all but the tips of their tail feathers turn white.

The white coat of the **Arctic fox** keeps the animal perfectly hidden as it creeps up on lemmings, its main prey. And this coat is also so long and dense that it may be the warmest of any animal fur.

Arctic gyrfalcons are large, powerful birds. They fly close to the ground in search of prey—usually other birds.

Even the **Arctic hare's** feet are covered with thick fur. This helps the hare's feet grip the slippery snow and keeps them warm as well. In summer, when the snows melt on the tundra, the hare's white fur turns brown.

The **ermine**, also known as the shorttail weasel, is almost pure white in winter. But when summer comes to the Arctic tundra, its thick coat turns brown.

Male **snowy owls** have spectacular white feathers, but females have many more dark, barred markings. Unlike most owls, the snowy owl hunts in the daytime, pouncing on lemmings, hares, and other small animals.

GUESS WHAT?...

Probably no animal lives farther north than the polar bear. The tracks of polar bears have been found only a mile or two from the North Pole.

One of the largest of all land hunters, the polar bear prowls the Arctic wilderness, searching for seals, its main prey. It often grabs the seals from their breathing holes in the ice.

Keeping warm

To escape from the bitter cold, the little **snow bunting** sometimes burrows into the snow. This bird nests farther north than any other bird.

THICK COATS of fur or feathers keep animals and birds that live in the coldest parts of the world warm. But cold water takes heat from an animal's body faster than air does, so sea-living polar creatures need more protection. They have layers of fatty blubber under their skin that keep them from losing too much body heat in icy seas.

The **eider duck** plucks warm, downy feathers from its breast to cover its eggs in the nest and prevent them from getting cold.

The musk ox's winter coat is longer than that of any other animal. Some of its thick hair is 3 feet long and reaches almost to the ground.

Under the outer coat of the musk ox is a thick layer of underfur that keeps out the cold and wet of the Arctic winter.

GUESS WHAT?...

Penguins, like the **chinstrap penguin**, have two layers of feathers as well as a layer of fatty blubber. The first layer of soft, downy feathers is covered by harder, oily feathers, which keep the penguin waterproof as well as warm.

Elephant seals are the biggest of all seals. A full-grown male can weigh up to 8,000 pounds—more than 40 or 50 humans. Once a year the elephant seal molts: it sheds its skin and hair and grows a sleek new coat.

A thick layer of fatty blubber keeps the **bowhead whale** warm in the coldest sea. Blubber accounts for nearly half the whale's weight.

Besides a layer of fatty blubber, the **walrus** has extremely thick skin. The blubber and skin together can be up to 6 inches thick—probably thicker than your whole body!

No trees survive on the tundra. But small plants, like the **creeping willow**, escape the bitter winds by growing close to the ground.

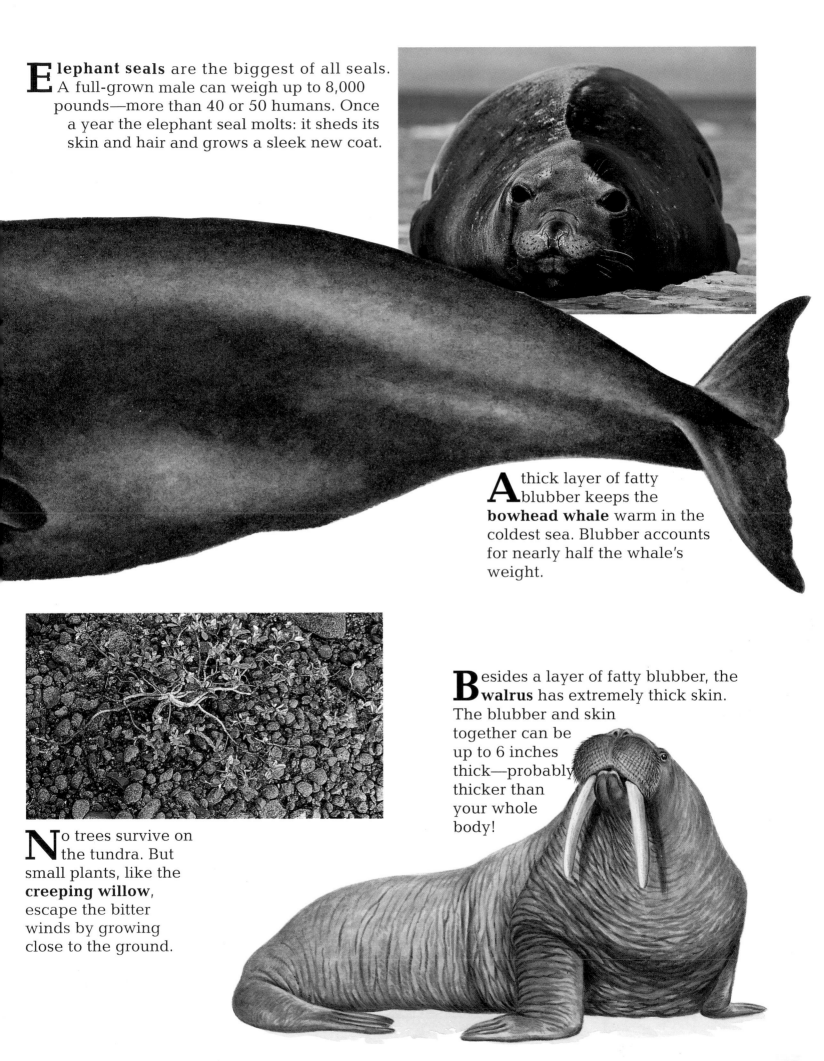

Life on the ice

THE ICY WASTES of the Arctic and the Antarctic do not look like comfortable homes, but some animals manage to live there all year round. There is always plenty of fish, shrimplike krill, and other shellfish for seals and the many types of polar birds to feed on. In the worst of the winter weather, seals spend most of their time in the sea, but in summer they haul themselves out onto the ice to bask in the sun.

The **ivory gull** follows polar bears and picks up the scraps from their meals as well as catching fish. It can run over the ice on its short, stumpy legs.

Gentoo penguins spend much of the winter in the sea, but in spring they trek across land to their breeding places on Antarctica. Penguins cannot fly, and the journey over the ice on foot may take many days.

Crabeater seals move fast over the ice, thrusting themselves forward with their front flippers. They may reach speeds of up to 15 miles an hour. Crabeaters are the most common type of seal in the Antarctic.

When penguins reach a slope, they often lie down on their bellies and "toboggan" over the snow, pushing themselves along with their flippers.

Ringed seals spend winter below the ice, coming to the surface at holes in the ice to breathe.

Under the ice

THE SEAS AROUND THE POLES teem with life. Temperatures in polar waters are more constant than land temperatures, and there are some warm currents. The smallest ocean life in the polar waters are the millions of tiny animals known as plankton.

Many kinds of fish also thrive in polar seas. Some of these have a sort of anti-freeze substance inside them that keeps their body fluids from turning to ice.

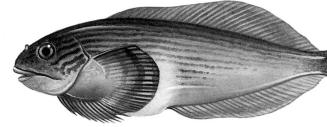

The **striped sea snail** has a little suction disk on its underside. With this, it can attach itself to the seabed or to seaweed.

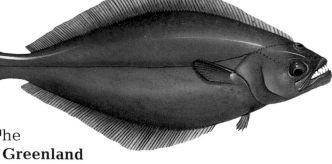

The **Greenland halibut** is a flatfish. Like all flatfishes it has both eyes on the right side of its body. It catches shellfish and squid in its strong, fanglike teeth.

GUESS WHAT?...

The icefish has blood that is almost transparent, not red like the blood of other creatures.

Icefish are the only creatures that have no oxygen-carrying red blood cells. A small amount of oxygen is carried in their blood, and because the fish are very sluggish, this is enough for their needs.

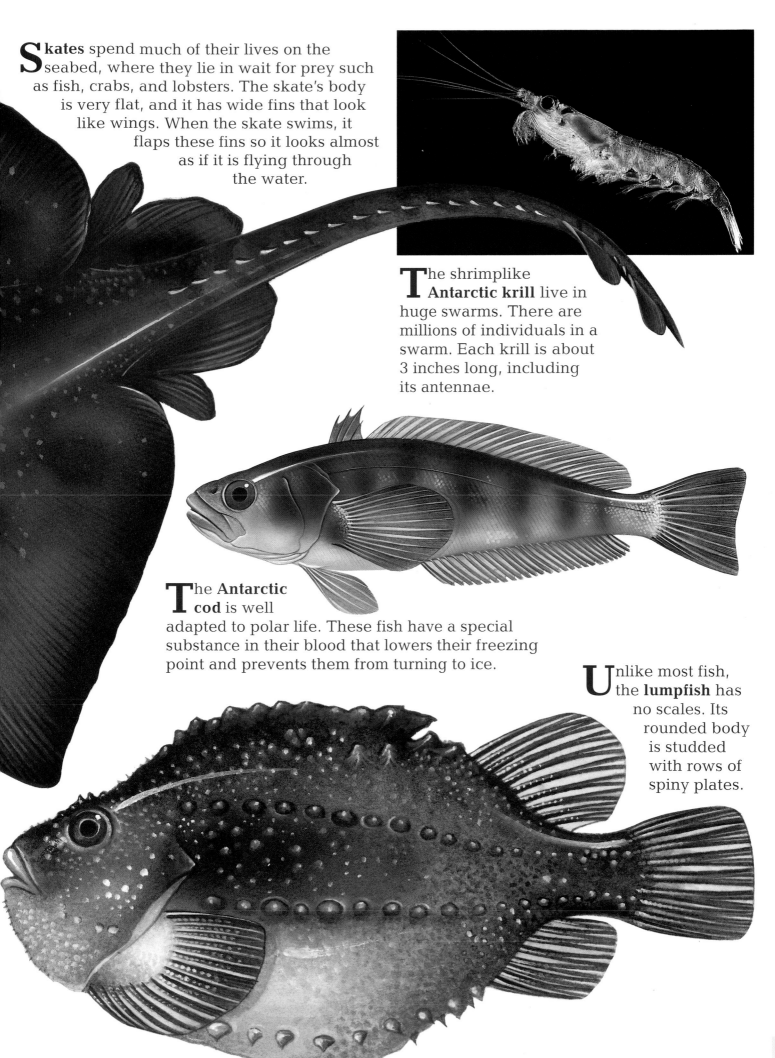

Skates spend much of their lives on the seabed, where they lie in wait for prey such as fish, crabs, and lobsters. The skate's body is very flat, and it has wide fins that look like wings. When the skate swims, it flaps these fins so it looks almost as if it is flying through the water.

The shrimplike **Antarctic krill** live in huge swarms. There are millions of individuals in a swarm. Each krill is about 3 inches long, including its antennae.

The **Antarctic cod** is well adapted to polar life. These fish have a special substance in their blood that lowers their freezing point and prevents them from turning to ice.

Unlike most fish, the **lumpfish** has no scales. Its rounded body is studded with rows of spiny plates.

Finding food

IN THE PARTS of the polar regions that are covered with snow all year round, the sea is the most important source of food for most animals. But on the Arctic tundra, where the snows melt each summer, animals can find food on land. As the ground thaws, new plants grow and flowers open, bringing plenty of leaves and seeds for plant eaters.

Warble flies are among the many insects that fill the air in the tundra summer. Their young, or larvae, live in and feed on the bodies of large animals like caribou.

King penguins dive deep in search of fish and squid. Most dives are down to about 160 feet, but king penguins have been known to plunge as deep as 800 feet—roughly the height of an 80-story building.

Young king penguin

The **puffin** seizes fish from the sea and carries it back to its nest in its large, strong beak. Puffins swim and dive well. Unlike penguins, they can fly.

Wilson's petrel hops and paddles over the surface of the ocean in search of shrimp and other shellfish. It often follows ships, picking up the creatures brought to the surface in the ship's wake.

The **leopard seal** is much slimmer than most seals and has a longer, more flexible neck. Built for speed, the leopard seal is a fierce hunter and snaps up young seals and penguins on the ice and under water.

The little **lemming** scurries along the ground searching for seeds and grass to eat. It will even dig beneath the snow to find food.

Snowy sheathbills eat almost anything they can find. They catch fish, seize the eggs and young from other birds' nests, and even visit the garbage cans of Antarctic science stations!

Arctic ground squirrels hibernate through the winter months. In the brief summer, they must eat plenty of roots, leaves, berries, and other plant material to build up their stores of body fat.

Hunters of the north

Great skuas do catch fish, but they also get much of their food by chasing other seabirds and forcing them to give up any food they are carrying.

IN THE FAR NORTH, animals that live by hunting must be adaptable, able to take advantage of any food that comes along. Animals such as wolves and wolverines attack creatures larger than themselves, but they will also pounce on a tiny mouse or fill up on berries. In such harsh conditions, animals cannot afford to be too choosy.

The male **narwhal** has a long tusk—actually a huge tooth—but it does not use the tusk for hunting. Some scientists think that the narwhal uses its tusk to battle with rival males for mates and territory.

Brown bears live in tundra areas and northern forests, where they hunt for small animals and fish. Bears will eat almost anything, however, and in late summer they gorge on fruit, nuts, and berries.

The **sable** hunts mice and other small creatures but also gobbles up any insects, nuts, berries, and honey that it can find.

Although a powerful hunter, the **wolverine** has short legs and is not a fast mover. It can catch animals larger than itself that have been slowed by deep snow. Alternatively, it hides and ambushes unsuspecting small animals and birds.

GUESS WHAT?...

Gray wolves are fierce hunters, but they live in close-knit family groups, or packs, and help each other hunt.

Working in groups of eight or more, gray wolves can bring down an animal as large as a musk ox, six or seven times their own weight.

On the tundra, wolves also hunt caribou, following the herds as they migrate in search of food.

The **hooded seal** dives deep to catch fish such as halibut and haddock. The male hooded seal has a special pouch of skin on its nose. This pouch can be blown up when the animal is alarmed or in danger, and the inflated "hood" then scares away an enemy or rival.

The fierce **killer whale** prowls Arctic coasts in search of fish, squid, seals, birds, and even other whales. Killer whales often swim in groups and hunt together.

Polar travelers

ANIMALS MIGRATE in order to get the best of two worlds. For many creatures, conditions in the Arctic are good in summer—there is plenty of food, and on the tundra the temperature even creeps above freezing. But at the end of the summer, many flee south to find winter food supplies and escape the cold.

Every fall, herds of **caribou** travel hundreds of miles from the tundra, where they live and breed in summer, to winter feeding areas farther south. Here the caribou feed mainly on lichens, scraping away the snow with their hooves to expose the plants. When spring comes, they return once more to the tundra.

The **golden plover** lays its eggs and rears its young on the tundra. In fall, it flies some 8,000 miles south to South America or to islands in the Pacific where it spends the winter.

In the fall, **gray whales** begin the 13,000-mile journey south to breeding areas in the Pacific Ocean—one of the longest migrations of any animal.

The **wandering albatross** spends most of its life soaring over the open ocean and Antarctic coasts. It migrates to islands in the southern oceans where it breeds, coming to land only to lay eggs and rear its young.

Canada geese lay their eggs and rear their young on the tundra. Entire families then fly south to the southern United States for the winter.

Beautiful white snow geese nest in colonies of thousands on the Arctic tundra. In winter they fly south, to areas like the Gulf of Mexico.

GUESS WHAT?...

The Arctic tern makes a round trip of about 20,000 miles each year— probably the longest migration of any bird.

Arctic terns lay their eggs in huge colonies on beaches and rocks during the Arctic summer. As winter approaches, the terns fly south all the way to the Antarctic in time for summer in the Southern Hemisphere.

Rearing young

Bellowing male **moose** lock antlers in fierce fights to win mates. The female gives birth to one calf, sometimes twins, which she feeds for about six months. The calf stays with its mother for about a year, until it has learned to fend for itself.

LIFE IS ALWAYS dangerous for young animals and birds, but nowhere is it more difficult than in the polar regions. Parents have to protect their babies against not only predators but also the extreme cold. The milk of some polar animals, like seals, is particularly fatty and rich so their young can grow quickly and get strong enough to survive the harsh conditions.

Some of the most devoted of all parents live at the Poles. Male emperor penguins don't eat for almost three months while they keep their eggs warm until they hatch.

Like all whales, the **white whale** gives birth to its young in the water. The mother takes very good care of her baby and feeds it for at least a year.

Southern **giant petrels** nest on the ground on Antarctic coasts and islands. If the nest is in danger, the petrel defends itself by spitting out bad-smelling oil from its beak. Even baby petrels can protect themselves this way.

Young petrels

The **tundra swan** lays her eggs in a nest of leaves and moss. The nest is lined with soft, downy feathers to help keep the eggs warm.

The emperor penguin must keep its egg warm through the bitter Antarctic winter.

The female emperor penguin lays her egg at the beginning of winter. Her mate then keeps the egg warm by rolling it onto his feet and covering it with a flap of skin on his belly. When the chick hatches, the male still keeps it safe on his feet for a few weeks.

Baby **harp seals** grow fast feeding on their mother's rich milk. When only two weeks old, the baby weighs three times as much as it did at birth and has a thick layer of blubber to protect it from the cold. Soon after this, the mother harp seal leaves her baby to fend for itself and find its own food.

Index

A
albatross, wandering, 5, 21

B
bear
    brown, 18
    polar, 4, 9
bunting, snow, 6, 10

C
caribou, 7, 20
cod, Antarctic, 15

D
duck, eider, 10

E
ermine, 4, 6, 9

F
fly, warble, 16
fox, Arctic, 4, 8

G
goose
    Canada, 21
    graylag, 4
    snow, 4, 21
gull, ivory, 12
gyrfalcon, 7, 9

H
halibut, Greenland, 14
hare, Arctic, 6, 9

I
icefish, 14

K
krill, Antarctic, 15

L
lemming, 6–7, 17
lumpfish, 15

M
moose, 22

N
narwhal, 4, 18

O
owl, snowy, 9
ox, musk, 7, 10

P
penguin
    Adélie, 5
    chinstrap, 5, 10
    emperor, 5, 23
    gentoo, 5, 12
    king, 5, 16
petrel
    southern giant, 22
    storm, 5
    Wilson's, 17
plover, golden, 20
ptarmigan, 4, 7, 8
puffin, 4, 17

S
sable, 18
seal
    crabeater, 13
    elephant, 5, 11
    fur, 5
    harp, 4, 23
    hooded, 19
    leopard, 17
    ringed, 13
sea snail, striped, 14
sheathbill, snowy, 17
skate, 15
skua, 5, 18
squirrel, Arctic ground, 7, 17
swan, tundra, 6, 23

T
tern, Arctic, 5, 21

W
walrus, 4, 11
weasel, shorttail, 9
whale
    bowhead, 11
    gray, 20
    killer, 5, 19
    white, 22
willow, creeping, 11
wolf
    Arctic, 4
    gray, 19
wolverine, 6, 18